SPRINGTIME
Find & Color

Agostino Traini

DOVER PUBLICATIONS, INC.
Mineola, New York

Copyright

Copyright © 2009 by Dover Publications, Inc.
All rights reserved.

Bibliographical Note

Springtime Find and Color is a new work, first published by Dover Publications, Inc., in 2009.

International Standard Book Number
ISBN-13: 978-0-486-47336-9
ISBN-10: 0-486-47336-8

Manufactured in the United States by Courier Corporation
47336802
www.doverpublications.com

Note

What comes to mind when you think of springtime? Do you think of flowers, singing birds, picnics, flying kites, or playing games outside? You'll find all this and much, much more in this unique find-and-color book! There are eighteen lively springtime scenes of everything from kids planting flowers in a garden, to an outdoor dance party, to a room full of Easter eggs, to a backyard barbeque, to sailboats! Share in all the excitement of spring as you "find and color" dozens of seasonal details. Each scene has a series of boxes that shows exactly what to look for in the pictures. If you can't find them all, just turn to page 38, where a Solutions section shows the correct answers. Now, get your colored pencils or markers ready, and have some springtime coloring fun!

11

24

Solutions

| 1 | 2 | 3 | 4 | 5 | 6 | 7 | 8 | 9 | 10 |

Pages 6-7

| 1 | 2 | 3 | 4 | 5 | 6 | 7 | 8 | 9 | 10 |

Pages 8-9

Pages 10-11

Pages 12-13

| 1 | 2 | 3 | 4 | 5 | 6 | 7 | 8 | 9 | 10 |

Pages 14-15

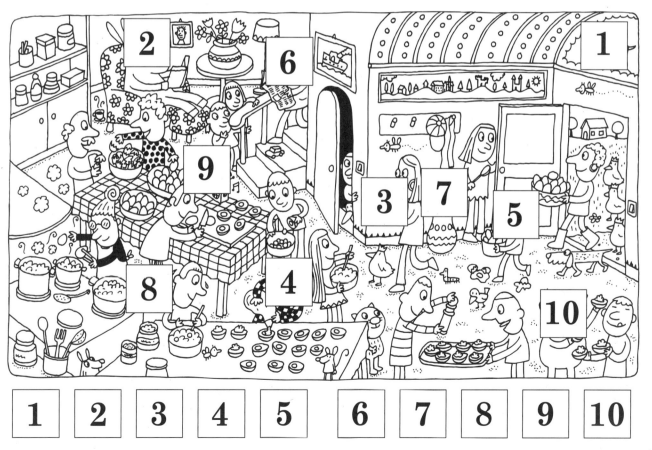

| 1 | 2 | 3 | 4 | 5 | 6 | 7 | 8 | 9 | 10 |

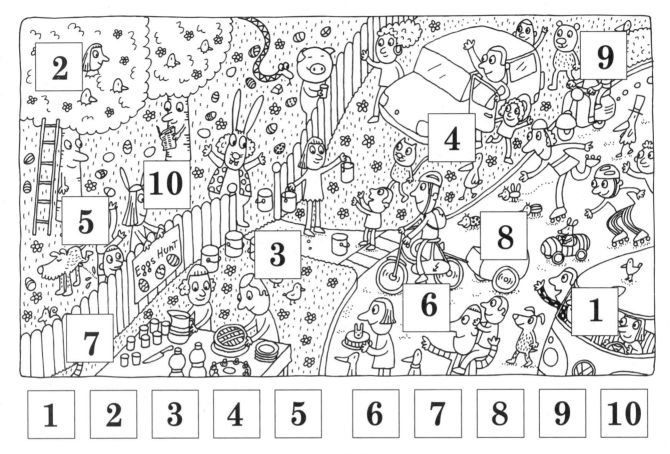

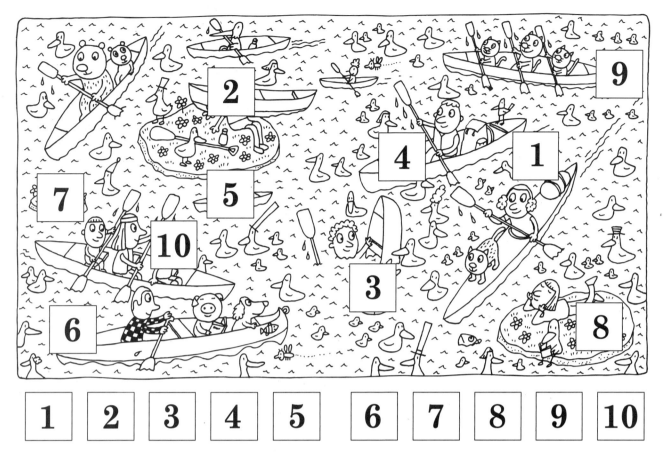

| 1 | 2 | 3 | 4 | 5 | 6 | 7 | 8 | 9 | 10 |

Pages 22-23

| 1 | 2 | 3 | 4 | 5 | 6 | 7 | 8 | 9 | 10 |

Pages 24-25

| 1 | 2 | 3 | 4 | 5 | 6 | 7 | 8 | 9 | 10 |

Pages 26-27

| 1 | 2 | 3 | 4 | 5 | 6 | 7 | 8 | 9 | 10 |

Pages 28-29

| 1 | 2 | 3 | 4 | 5 | 6 | 7 | 8 | 9 | 10 |

Pages 30-31

| 1 | 2 | 3 | 4 | 5 | 6 | 7 | 8 | 9 | 10 |

Pages 32-33

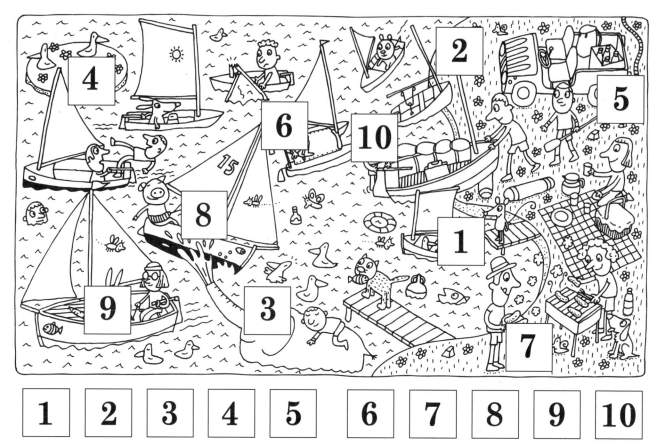

$$\boxed{1} \quad \boxed{2} \quad \boxed{3} \quad \boxed{4} \quad \boxed{5} \quad \boxed{6} \quad \boxed{7} \quad \boxed{8} \quad \boxed{9} \quad \boxed{10}$$

Pages 34-35

$$\boxed{1} \quad \boxed{2} \quad \boxed{3} \quad \boxed{4} \quad \boxed{5} \quad \boxed{6} \quad \boxed{7} \quad \boxed{8} \quad \boxed{9} \quad \boxed{10}$$

Pages 36-37